The Antique Dealer's Guide to

Facebook Marketplace

SELLING VINTAGE AND ANTIQUES ON MARKETPLACE

By

KATHY TODD

The Antique Dealer's Guide to Facebook Marketplace

Selling Vintage and Antiques on Marketplace

Kathy Todd

Lafayette and Rose Press

ISBN: 978-1-7366204-1-0

TABLE OF CONTENTS

INTRODUCTION

Collecting antiques is a hobby that many people enjoy. At some point though, you made the decision the transition from buying antiques to selling them. Maybe you started by selling off pieces of your collection as your tastes became more refined and you no longer wanted the more common pieces in your collection. You wanted to make space and provide funds to purchase pieces that were more valuable and rare. Or maybe you decided you have a real eye for antiques and you wanted to turn your hobby into a profitable business. Or perhaps your decision came from the encouragement and recognition of a friend or family member that saw that you have a gift or passion for antiques.

As an antique dealer you have probably been selling your inventory through traditional channels such as antique stores or malls, at local markets, or online through venues such as Etsy or eBay. Each of these resources offers a variety of benefits. That's how I got started.

I opened my first booth in 2014 at a local antique mall. I thoroughly enjoyed having a booth and the experience of learning how to successfully operate an antique business. There was much trial and error, from learning what kinds of items would attract customers in my market, to learning how to best display the items to make my booth appealing to customers. It was a fun, educational, and profitable experience.

However, having a booth wasn't my first experience with selling antiques. I opened an eBay shop in the year 2000 and I still buy and sell on that site today. More recently though (2017), I opened an Etsy shop for selling vintage and antique items. With careful research, and again, much trial and error, I was able to determine which items sold best in each venue.

During the time that I had my antique booth, I discovered Facebook Marketplace. At first, I was a little hesitant to use it. The reason why was primarily safety concerns, both personal and financial. I didn't want to have buyers come to my home and I was also uncomfortable meeting with them by myself in a public location. I was also concerned about the possibility of being scammed.

When I first started selling on Facebook Marketplace, I was extra cautious. I would often ask my husband to meet with the buyer at an agreed upon location. Sometimes I would go with him, but not always. This worked great when he wasn't too busy with his work, but it got to the point that he couldn't always do it for me and I didn't want to continue taking up his time with my business. Since we had never had any problems with any of my customers, I gradually became more comfortable with meeting them by myself.

I started using Facebook Marketplace about four years ago when I still had my antique booth. I found it to be a great way to promote the items that were in my booth to a larger audience. Since closing my booth, I have continued using Marketplace to sell a variety of vintage and antique items. It has been a learning process and I am going to share with you how you can best use Marketplace to sell your vintage and antique pieces.

Facebook Marketplace has many features that make it ideal for selling antiques (or almost anything else for that matter). Some of the benefits include:

- It is extremely mobile friendly.

- You don't have to ship your items (as long as you sell using the Local Pickup Only option).

- They don't charge you fees when you sell your items (at least not at the time this book was published, and as long as you are selling locally and using the Local Pickup Only option and not shipping the items).

Most people use smartphones these days and Facebook has made it easy to use your phone to create your listings. Everything can be done on your phone and everything I cover in this book is based on using your phone to create and manage your listings on Marketplace.

- You will take photos with your phone.

- You will create the listings with your phone.

- You will communicate with your customers, using Facebook Messenger, on your phone.

Learning to use Facebook Marketplace is relatively easy. Once you get started, I think you will enjoy the process and you will definitely enjoy the increased sales that will come as a result of reaching a larger audience who have very specific interests in items such as yours.

Note: Facebook Marketplace periodically changes and updates its rules and regulations. While the step-by-step instructions included in this book may be modified by Facebook at some point in the future, the general information and guidance shared here will still apply.

This book is intended to help you learn and feel comfortable with the process of promoting and selling antiques on Facebook Marketplace. I wish you much success with growing your business.

CHAPTER 1

WHY SHOULD I SELL ON FACEBOOK MARKETPLACE?

If you have already been selling on platforms such as Etsy and eBay, or you have an antique booth where you sell your merchandise, you are going to be pleased with how much easier (and more profitable) it can be to sell the exact same items on Facebook Marketplace (I will refer to it as Marketplace from this point forward.). Not only is it easier, but you also don't have listing/selling fees or booth rental/commission costs (as long as you sell locally and don't ship the item). And it is not an all or nothing deal. You can use Marketplace to enhance and promote what you already have for sale in your antique booth. You can also cross post your Etsy and eBay listings on Marketplace. Marketplace will give you a lot more flexibility at no additional cost.

Facebook launched Marketplace in 2016 as a way for individuals to sell their personal items in a social media environment. While it was first started as a place to sell to friends and family, it later expanded to allow businesses to also sell their products. This book will focus on selling as an individual.

Are You Ready to Give It a Try?

Marketplace is an ideal place for selling antiques and the process is easy to learn. The first step you will need to take is to think about what you have to sell. Do you have a piece that has just been sitting in your booth or your online shop for a while? A piece that you are tired of looking at or is one that is simply taking up too much space? Well, why not start with that one? If you are a booth owner, I am sure you know the importance of keeping your booth fresh. Shoppers will walk right by your booth if it looks exactly the same as it did the last time they were in the store. If you have a piece that has not garnered much interest from your regular customers, then it may be time to branch out and reach new potential buyers and finally get that piece sold.

One of the nicest things about selling pieces from your booth through Marketplace is that you don't even have to meet in person with the customer. Not that you necessarily mind meeting with your customers, it's just that it can be a hassle for both of you to coordinate your time, their time, and the hours that your store is open. But if you let them know that they can view your item in your antique booth, then all you have to do is let them know your store name, location, and booth number.

They can stop by the store during business hours and buy it at a time that is convenient for them.

Another advantage of selling through Marketplace is the fact that it is a social marketplace. You have the ability to see potential buyers' profiles, any mutual friends, and even their ratings/reviews from other sellers.

Reach Specific/Targeted Customers

Marketplace enables you to reach very specific customers. Think about it; say you have a set of vintage Lenox china that has been sitting in your booth for months with absolutely no interest. If you list it on Marketplace and someone who registered for that pattern thirty years ago when they got married but never completed purchasing it finds it on Marketplace, they will be thrilled, and you will have an easy sale. The odds of that same customer just happening to walk into your antique mall and finding their way to your booth and locating a discontinued china pattern that they have been searching for is highly unlikely.

This exact scenario actually happened to me. I had a beautiful set of vintage china that had sat in my booth for months. I finally decided to list it on Marketplace. In this instance, I had already taken the set of china out of my booth (to free up space for other pieces) and photographed and created the listing at my home. I met the buyer at a local gas station. She was so excited to get these dishes. She said she had seen them many years ago and couldn't afford them at the time. She was probably in her seventies. She was so happy to finally be able to buy them and I was happy to finally sell them and free up some space in my antique booth. It was definitely a win-win situation.

I have listed large pieces of furniture that were taking up a significant amount of space in my booth for months. The pieces obviously didn't appeal to the customers in my store, but they sold quickly to Marketplace buyers and freed up valuable floor space in my booth.

Selling a Wider Variety of Items

Another thing to consider is that you can sell a wider variety of items on Marketplace. Most successful antique booths have a cohesive look and feel. Aesthetically, mid-century modern and Victorian pieces do not mix well with one another. Customers prefer a booth that displays items that go together. So, if you have a nice mid-century piece that won't work in your Victorian booth then Marketplace might be the perfect place to sell it.

The store where I had my antique booth was full of very traditional antiques. When I would put a mid-century piece in my booth it would just sit for months and months. There is a huge demand for mid-century pieces in other areas and these same pieces would sell quickly when I listed them on Marketplace.

Most antique dealers are constantly looking for pieces to go in their booths or online shops. Sometimes you run across items that are such a good deal that you just can't leave them behind. When it is time to put it in your shop though, you realize that it just doesn't go with the other types of items you are selling. Sometimes too, you end up buying an "auction lot" that consists of things that you want for your booth, but which also includes items that don't work with your current booth or online shop style. Marketplace is an excellent venue for selling the profitable items that just don't fit in your current shop.

Even if you have a booth and sell on platforms such as eBay and Etsy, Marketplace can greatly increase the number of potential customers you can reach and enable you to sell your inventory more quickly.

CHAPTER 2

WHERE SHOULD I SELL: MARKETPLACE, ANTIQUE BOOTH, OR ETSY/EBAY?

As a seller of vintage and antique items (I will just use the term antique from this point forward.), you have likely become quite comfortable with your selling venue. Perhaps you sell small items or things (smalls) on Etsy or eBay, or you have a diverse collection of large and small items in an antique booth. Regardless of which of these venues you use, there are pros and cons to each. If you spend some time thinking about how you sell, you may discover that it could quite possibly work to your advantage to offer your items for sale in more than one venue. It will require you to keep careful track of your inventory, but it should help you increase sales.

In addition to being comfortable with your selling venue, you have probably reached a level of expertise with the venue that you are using and may not be sure how to incorporate

Marketplace into your business plan. Also, you may think that if what you are doing is working, then why try something else? Consider the following:

- What if something else works better?

- Shortens your sales cycle?

- Increases your profit?

- Increases your visibility to potential new customers?

- Brings new customers to your shop (either your in-person or online shop)?

If any of these things are the case, then you should definitely consider adding Marketplace to your sales strategies.

Selling Items from Your Antique Booth

Some things just seem to be a natural fit for selling in an antique booth. Furniture is a great example. It is large and bulky, it can be easily scratched or scuffed if moved too often, and it is often difficult and too heavy to move on your own. Once you place it in your booth, you really don't want to have to move it again. It isn't too difficult to move it around your booth, but you don't want to have to bring it home or put it in a storage unit because it hasn't sold.

One great thing about furniture is that it can be so versatile in an antique booth. Once you have it staged in your booth, it can make an attractive backdrop for your other items. It can also anchor your booth and balance out smaller items. If it is a bookcase or a china cabinet, then it can offer a large amount of display space.

On the other hand though, larger pieces can certainly take up a lot of space and if the pieces you have selected turn out to be unpopular in your area, they can take a while to sell.

Unfortunately, if this is the case and you have furniture that has been sitting in your booth for months, then your booth can start to look stale, and you may start to lose the interest of regular customers in your store. People like to see new things and if they have been in your store recently and your booth looks almost exactly the same as it did since the last time they were there, then they might just walk right by your booth without even giving it a second glance. This is one thing that many antique mall owners emphasize. As they sit there day after day watching customers and their shopping habits, they have noticed that buyers are attracted to the booths that have been updated and refreshed with new merchandise and they walk right by the ones that rarely change. If you are tired of looking at it, then your customers might be too.

Dealing with low turnover in your antique booth inventory can be quite frustrating. It is difficult for a booth owner to make changes and refresh their booth when things aren't selling. Sure, you might like to bring in some new pieces, but you really don't want to take home something that has been sitting for a while in your booth, especially if it is bulky or heavy. However, if you are able to regularly sell the large items from your booth each month (or each week), then your booth could potentially have a new look every time your frequent customers come in, thus making it more appealing and resulting in more sales. Knowing that your booth is the one that has something new/different each time will make customers return to a store just to visit your booth. If it is in a large antique mall, they may even skip walking up and down all the other aisles and just go straight to your booth. I usually shop the entire store when I visit my local antique mall because I am always looking for a bargain. However, if I don't have a lot of time that day, I will just go to my favorite booths that are always being updated.

Using Marketplace to promote the items in your booth can help you get them sold more quickly. Sometimes you, and the store where you have your booth, can get in a rut, especially when things are slow. When the antique store where I used to have multiple booths started promoting items on Marketplace, it generated a lot of attention and increased sales. Once more things started going out of the store, vendors were able to bring in new items to sell and we had new customers, many of whom had never even heard of our store before.

When I started using Marketplace to promote new items in my own booth, I began to get new customers, and not just lookers. They were customers who were in my booth to specifically buy an item that I had for sale. I would simply list the item on Marketplace and include the store information (and my booth number) in the ad, and the customers would come in and make their purchases at a time that was convenient for them.

In addition, I would let the store owner know that I had just listed something on Marketplace. That way if the customer happened to forget my booth number, the store employee would hopefully remember that I called and then be able to direct them to my booth. Remember, if you are in a large antique mall, you really can't expect store employees to know where every single item is located. It can be too much for them to keep up with. However, by just giving them a quick call to inform them of a potential buyer, you improve the experience for both your buyer and the store employee. It also keeps the buyer focused on your item. You don't want them wandering the aisles and potentially purchasing someone else's item.

One of the best things that I found about this method was the convenience it provided for both me and my customers. We didn't have to set up a time or neutral/safe location to meet. They could simply go into the antique store during normal business hours and purchase the item at a time that was convenient for them.

This was especially nice when dealing with large furniture. Typically, if you are trying to sell furniture from your home, your customer will need to meet with you at your home. You are not likely to want to load up the furniture and take it somewhere to meet a customer. You may also have to help them load the furniture into their vehicle. Waiting on them to show up and then helping them load the furniture can be time consuming and hard on your back. Directing them to your antique booth on the other hand, requires very little effort on your part.

Selling on Etsy or eBay

Some items are just a natural fit for Etsy or eBay. For example, I am currently selling individual pieces of a collection of Kunstlerschutz flocked animal figurines. Most people have never even heard of these collectibles. I certainly hadn't until I purchased the collection at an estate sale and took them home to research.

Kunstlerschutz animal figurines were made in the German town of Rodental between the 1940s and 1960s. Each animal figurine was made by hand from paper and clay and then covered with cotton fibers (flocked). Some of these figurines are quite rare now and there are not a lot of buyers for them. However, the buyers who are interested in them are often willing to pay a premium price. Finding these specific buyers is a challenge. You are much more likely to find buyers for this type of item using sites such as eBay or Etsy, which have huge numbers of customers who come to these sites to specifically search for rare items.

Another advantage to selling an item like these flocked animal figurines on eBay or Etsy is that they are very easy to ship. They aren't breakable, so you can simply put them in a small box and take them to the post office.

However, what if you have a beautiful set of antique Limoges china? You could possibly sell it for a higher price on eBay or Etsy, but it would be a major hassle (and expense by the time you purchase bubble wrap, boxes, and other packing material) to ship and even with careful and thorough packaging, there would be a chance that some of the pieces might arrive broken. I can't tell you how many times I have had packages arrive at my home with huge dents in them. Sometimes they are just tossed halfway down the driveway and not even delivered to my covered porch. If that happens to one of your eBay or Etsy customers, then they will likely demand a full or partial refund. Also, if they decide to send it back to you then you would probably be responsible for paying the return shipping costs. After refunding the purchase price, paying to ship it back, and losing the commission, you could be out a significant amount of money (after putting in a lot of work).

If you sell a fine china set like this on Marketplace though, you can arrange to meet your customer somewhere close to your home. You will still have to box up the pieces, but they won't have to be wrapped as thoroughly as they would if you were shipping them. Also, you won't have to worry about buyer's remorse. Once you receive payment from the customer, then the deal is done. Just make sure you give them the opportunity to thoroughly inspect the item before you conclude the deal and collect payment.

Some buyers are very polite and simply take the item from me once they have paid for it. I always encourage them to look closely at the item or pieces included in a set to make sure they are happy with it. This is important for both parties. Once, when I was the customer, I drove a fairly long way to purchase a set of china. They had it neatly boxed and ready to go. Even though the sellers were very nice, and the china was neatly packaged, I went ahead and unwrapped a piece to check it out. It was the wrong pattern! They had made a mistake in the listing and had it listed with the wrong name. I was so glad I checked it out. I sure would have been disappointed when I got home if I hadn't taken the time to unwrap a piece of it. I think oftentimes people are reluctant to look at the item when they meet you in person because they are worried they will offend you. That is their decision, but you should always offer them the opportunity.

Selling Items with Minor Damage/Flaws

If you sell on Etsy or eBay, then you know how picky customers can be. The slightest flaw (often ones that you may not even have noticed) can result in negative feedback and a demand for a refund from your customer.

I once sold an Eastern Airlines model airplane on eBay. The customer noticed a hole in the plane that was the size of a pin head. I inspect things very thoroughly before I ship them, but I hadn't noticed it because it was so tiny. He was right though. It had a tiny hole in it. I told him to just keep it and I refunded his money. I knew that after paying return shipping costs that my losses would be even greater, so I just let him keep it. In the end, I lost the price of the item, the eBay fees, and the cost of shipping. If I had sold this through Marketplace though, the buyer could have inspected it and if he had noticed the flaw, we could have negotiated a lower price and we would have both been happy.

Just because something may have a small chip or minor paint loss doesn't mean it should go in the trash heap. A couple of years ago I bought a large collection of vintage Fostoria American crystal. Most of the pieces were in excellent condition but some of them did have minor flaws. I was able to sell both the perfect and damaged pieces.

Why would someone buy a damaged antique? Certain pieces are so desirable and so rare that some customers want them despite the flaws. Another reason a customer might want a slightly damaged piece is because it is much more affordable than one in perfect condition. While a Fostoria American square puff box might sell for more than five hundred dollars if it is in mint condition, the same box with a small chip in the lid might sell for one hundred dollars or even less.

I am an avid collector of McCoy pottery planters and vases. While I prefer pieces that are in perfect condition, if I come across a piece that I find particularly appealing or one that I know is hard to find, I will still buy it even if it has a minor flaw, especially if the flawed area isn't that noticeable. If I were looking for pieces to resell I might not purchase it, but I would definitely consider it for my own collection if the piece were one that I really wanted and the flaw was small and not that noticeable.

Even though you may disclose damage in an eBay listing, the problem is that many customers don't read the description closely enough. Although you may have disclosed the damage in both the title and the description, they can still say that it was worse than you described and ask for their money back. As you may know, eBay and Etsy usually side with the buyers. This can become very costly to you when you have to refund the purchase price, as well as shipping costs both ways. Sometimes you may decide it is not worth the cost of shipping it back and you simply let the customer keep the item (or even worse, eBay tells them they can keep the item). When this is the case, you are out the purchase price and shipping costs, and you no longer have the item. The cost of these failed transactions can really add up.

With Marketplace, you have the opportunity to allow your customer to evaluate the item when they purchase it. They can then decide if they are satisfied with the quality. I always ask my customers to look over an item before I collect the money for it. If you conduct your business in person and make sure the customer is satisfied before accepting their money, then you don't have to worry about them asking for refunds.

Once I sold a pair of beautiful pink pottery vases on Marketplace. I met with the buyer and she began examining them very closely. After running her finger over the surface of one of the vases she found a small chip that someone had actually colored in with a pink marker to disguise it. She still wanted the vases, but I felt bad that I had sold her something without disclosing the damage (I hadn't noticed the damage.). I gave her a partial refund even though she didn't ask for it and said it wasn't necessary. It felt necessary to me though because I knew the vases weren't worth as much with the damage.

Tips for Selling on Multiple Venues

While not everyone may agree with me on this, I believe that it is a good idea to list your items for sale on multiple venues. The main reason people may not want to do so is that you run the risk of double selling your item. However, if you carefully manage your listings and end the listings as soon as they sell on one site, then it can definitely help you sell things sooner. As I mentioned above, you can list an item on Marketplace and simply tell potential customers to go to your store to purchase it.

If you have an item listed on eBay or Etsy, go ahead and list it locally on Marketplace too. By doing so you are increasing the number of people that see your item for sale. Some things, such as the Kunstlerschutz animals, are more likely to sell through Etsy or eBay since they generally only appeal to a very specific buyer, but you just might luck up and find a local collector. It only takes that one right buyer.

If you do find a local buyer through Marketplace, then you will be saving money on eBay/Etsy fees, as well as PayPal fees. In addition, you will be avoiding the hassles involved with shipping. Also, you don't have to worry about customers asking for refunds (up to thirty days later).

Just remember though, once you sell something on Marketplace, you need to immediately remove the listing from anywhere else you have it listed. You don't want it to sell twice and then have to deal with angry customers and negative ratings. Plus, it will just make things easier overall for you.

Using multiple venues to promote your items is a great marketing strategy. You never know who might be looking for an item exactly like yours on Marketplace. It can be a very satisfying feeling to provide someone with a special piece that they will use themselves or share with a family member.

Last year I had an old icebox for sale on Marketplace. It had the name of a local dairy on the front of the box. I sold it to a man who had the same last name as the dairy. I asked him if his family had owned that dairy. He said no but since it had his family name on it, he wanted to buy it for his parents for Christmas. He said they didn't really need anything at their age, but he thought they would truly treasure such a unique item with their family name on it. He was so excited to purchase it and I have to say I was very glad that I could make that happen for him.

CHAPTER 3

WHAT CANNOT BE SOLD ON MARKETPLACE

Facebook's Commerce Policies provide details on what you can and cannot sell on Marketplace. You should take the time to review these policies. In addition to following Facebook's policies, you will also need to comply with all applicable laws and regulations for your area.

You need to take Facebook's rules seriously. Failure to comply with their rules can result in the removal of your listing, or for more serious or repeated violations, suspension of your access to Facebook.

Prohibited Items

The following products are prohibited from being sold on Marketplace.

- Adult products

- Alcohol

- Animals

- Body parts or fluids

- Digital media and electronic devices

- Discrimination-related items

- Documents (fake), currency, and financial instruments

- Gambling

- Hazardous goods and materials

- Human exploitation and sexual services

- Ingestible supplements

- Jobs

- Medical and healthcare products

- Anything misleading, violent, or hateful

- No item for sale

- Prescription products, drugs, or drug paraphernalia

- Products with overtly sexual positioning

- Recalled products

- Services

- Stolen goods

- Subscriptions and digital products

- Third-party infringement

- Tobacco products and related paraphernalia

- Used cosmetics

- Weapons, ammunition, and explosives

How Does This Apply to the Sale of Antiques?

You may be thinking that many of these categories are not antiques so why bother listing them here. The reason is because Facebook uses a proprietary artificial intelligence system to review your listings before they are published to the site. Basically, it uses an automated computer program to review your listings. Instead of people determining if your listings meet the requirements of their Commerce Policies, Facebook has developed a computer program that scans all your listings.

If you are still wondering why you should care, it is because their system can make mistakes. Say for example you have a painting of a gun used during the Civil War, most of the time the Marketplace review system will recognize that your item is a painting but sometimes it will not let you post it because it considers your painting to be a "weapon."

A few years ago, I listed a beautiful painting of some cows in a pasture. It was rejected by Facebook because you can't sell livestock. More recently, I listed a collection of vintage dog figurines, and it was also rejected because you can't sell any kind of live animal. If an actual person had reviewed these listings, I am confident they would have been approved. Dealing with Facebook's "technology" can be challenging, but it is just part of the process.

Appealing Facebook's Decision

If your listing has been rejected by Facebook for violation of its Commerce Policies, they will allow you to appeal the decision. Appealing the decision is easy to do. It may take them a while to respond though. It can be frustrating because they won't always tell you what you did wrong. They simply refer you to their Commerce Policies.

If your listing has been rejected, go to the search bar in Marketplace and enter Commerce Policies. It will take you to a page that details what is not allowed on Marketplace. Read through this page and see if you can determine which policy you may have violated. Once you have figured it out, make changes to your listing and then try listing it again.

If you still can't figure out why they have rejected your listing and you think that it does not violate their Commerce Policies, then you can file an appeal. Go to Facebook Help and search for Marketplace Item Appeal. Complete the form and wait for their response.

If they still don't approve your listing, then you will need to delete it and start over. Be sure and word it differently (the title and the description) and use at least a few different photos and try listing it again. This usually works.

Community Standards

In addition to adhering to the Commerce Policies, all listings must adhere to Facebook's Community Standards. These standards are in place to make sure that listings are respectful and not offensive to anyone looking at your listing. They focus on safety, objectionable content, violence and criminal behavior, integrity, authenticity, and respecting intellectual content.

CHAPTER 4

CREATING A LISTING

Now that you have decided to take the plunge and have identified items that you want to sell on Marketplace (and you know what you can't sell), it is time to create your first listing. Facebook has made this process quite easy to do and it is very mobile friendly. By mobile friendly I mean you don't have to crack open your laptop or desktop at all to create your listings. I create all my listings on my smartphone, and it is a quick and simple process.

Take Great Photos

Taking great photos is an important first step. When a potential customer searches for an item to purchase, Marketplace presents them with a list of items that meet their search criteria. Each of the items listed includes a photo of the item. Buyers are naturally drawn to items with the most appealing photos. Unless they have a specific budget that they can't exceed, people are more likely to choose an item based on the photos in the listings. Chapter 6 provides more information on how to take great photos for your listings.

Follow the Step-by-Step Process

Creating a Marketplace listing is relatively easy. As I mentioned earlier, all instructions included in this book are based on using your smartphone for creating your listings. Also note, Facebook periodically changes how things work on their site so the instructions may change from what I have included here at some point in the future. However, if that is the case, just follow the step-by-step process that Facebook provides.

To create a listing, click on the shop/Marketplace icon at the bottom of the screen on your phone. This will take you to Marketplace. Follow the steps below to create your listing.

1. Click on the Selling button at the top of the page.

2. Click Create New Listing.

3. Choose the type of item that you want to sell. For antiques, select Items.

4. Click Add Your Photos to add photos from your phone. This will take you to the photos you have saved on your phone. Select the photos you want to use in the order that you want them to appear. (Facebook will crop your photos to fit their format so you may have to experiment with your

own cropping to make sure the item displays the way you want it to in the listing.)

5. Enter your title. You don't know what words buyers will use in their search so use as many descriptive words as possible. For example, if you are listing an antique armoire, you will obviously use armoire, but also use wardrobe, linen press, and any other words that you think might be used to describe the item. Include the materials that it is made from such as walnut, cherry, or oak. Include the style such as French Country, Classic Regency, or Primitive. Try and think of all the different ways a person might identify and try to search for your item.

6. Enter your price. I will cover more details about pricing in Chapter 10.

7. Select a category. I normally select the first category, Antiques and Collectibles.

8. Select the condition. It is important to be honest here. If it is not as good as new, then don't say it is. Your buyer will know this as soon as he sees the item. (See tip at the end of the chapter.)

9. Enter the description. This is your opportunity to really sell your item. Start with a general description that covers the basics and then go into greater detail. People prefer listings with thorough descriptions. If they are going to go to the effort to meet you to purchase an item, they want to make

sure it is exactly what they want. After I have written a thorough description, I copy and paste the text that I entered in the title and add that to the description. This will ensure that all key words from the title are included in the description. Chapter 11 explains how to write great product descriptions.

10. Add your location. You will only have to do this once. This won't give out your specific address. It just gives buyers a general idea of where you are located.

11. Select a delivery method. I have my Marketplace profile set up with Local Pickup Only. This keeps things simple and works great for me since many of the items that I list on Marketplace would be difficult to ship. While Marketplace has purchase protection policies in place for buyers, they don't really offer any type of protection for sellers. Facebook also allows buyers to create a claim up to 45 days from the date an item is delivered. Since there is always a greater potential for scamming to take place when shipping items, I rarely do this. Also, you run the risk of items getting damaged during shipping.

12. The next screen allows you to pick additional Facebook groups where you can share your listing. Groups can be very specific either to a location or topic/item. Listing your items in group will give them a lot more exposure to audiences who are very interested in that specific type of item.

This is another particularly important step that you need to put some effort into, and I will give you more details about groups in the following chapter.

13. That's it. Click Publish and you are done. You have listed your first item on Marketplace. Now gather some more antiques and start listing them too.

Sharing on Your Personal Page

Marketplace gives you the option to share your listing on your personal page. This is something that I choose not to do. I like to keep my personal and business information separate from one another. Keep in mind though that even if you don't share the listing on your personal page, some of your Facebook friends may see your listing if they are searching for something similar. Also keep this in mind if you are trying to sell something that someone gave you as a gift. You wouldn't want them to see your listing on Marketplace.

Tip: Be honest about the condition of the item you are trying to sell. If a potential buyer clicks on your listing and sees that you have described the item condition as new, but they can tell from the photos that it is not in new condition, then that is not going to make a good impression. They will automatically become suspicious of everything in your listing because you weren't honest about the condition. Don't make this mistake.

If you feel that it is in good condition for its age, then say that. You can also say things such as, "This item is in very good condition for its age. It has normal wear and tear as would be expected for its age," or something similar. I don't think anyone expects something that is one hundred years old to be in perfect condition, so just describing it accurately will make you more credible as a seller.

CHAPTER 5

FACEBOOK GROUPS

If you have been active on Facebook for a while, then it is likely that you have joined some groups. Facebook groups are a place to communicate about shared interests with other members. There are groups for just about any interests. Not only are they a great resource for selling, but they are also an excellent resource for learning more about whatever that group focuses on.

I am a member of quite a few groups including ones that focus on Fostoria glass, ephemera, buying and selling antiques, selling on eBay and Etsy, Hull pottery, antique typewriters, Lefton figurines, and many more. These groups are excellent resources for researching antiques and collectibles. Many of the members are passionate about their collections and are usually eager to share their knowledge.

In addition to joining groups that focus on specific types of items, you should also join local buying and selling groups.

Search for and join local city, county, region, and state groups that focus on buying and selling. Some of these groups allow you to sell anything (that is allowed by Facebook), and others focus on a specific type of item such as furniture, antiques, or porcelain.

Many Facebook groups allow you to sell your antiques on their group pages. However, some groups have very specific rules about how you can list things for sale, and they can be quite strict. Some of them will delete your listings if you don't follow their rules exactly. If you break their rules more than a couple of times, they might even remove you from their group. Good manners are important in these groups, and as long as you follow their rules, they can be an excellent place to sell your antiques.

Increase Views by Joining Groups

As I mentioned in the previous section, Marketplace gives you the option to list your item in additional groups. This is a valuable option because it can get your antiques a lot more views, and the views are specific to viewers interested in the type of item that you are listing.

Facebook groups are a great resource for antique collectors because they can be used for a number of things related to antiques. For example, many groups focus on helping their members identify antiques. There are antique clock groups, antique jewelry groups, antique railroad collectible groups, and many, many more. There are groups for just about any topic you can think of. The information that you can learn in these groups can be quite helpful to you as an antique dealer. Facebook groups can help you with both sales and specific information about all kinds of antiques.

One of the Fostoria American groups that I am a member of is a great example of a Facebook group that provides helpful/educational information to its members. Fostoria American pieces can be quite valuable. However, there are other brands, such as Whitehall, that look almost identical to the Fostoria American pieces. This group has very knowledgeable members who will take the time to describes and provide visual examples of how to tell the difference between American and Whitehall pieces.

Some groups are public and once you find them you simply click on the Join button. Other groups are private and require that you apply to join them. They will often make you answer three or four questions to determine if you are a good fit for their group. It's a pretty easy process and it doesn't usually take long to hear back from them. Many of them only ask that you read and follow their rules.

Remember though, you have to be a member of a group before you can post your items to sell in those groups.

Finding Groups to Join

Finding groups to join is easy. Click on the Menu at the bottom of the page. Select Groups and then click the search icon (magnifying glass) in the top right corner. Type in a word such as "antique" or "ephemera" in the search bar at the top of your Facebook home page. As you start typing your word, it will give you a list of possible groups to join. Go ahead and click on one of them. Once you are on their page, read the description and if it interests you then click Join.

After you join a group or request to join a group, Facebook will suggest other groups that might interest you. Just keep joining groups until you feel like you have covered all your areas of interest. In addition to helping you with your Marketplace listings, groups are a great educational resource. You can talk to other experts and enthusiasts about your favorite antiques and ask questions in the groups. Some groups will help you determine the value of your antiques (Read the group rules first though because some groups do not allow price discussions.). You can even ask group members if there are any other groups that they would recommend.

Once you have joined some groups, they will appear in the List in Other Places section when you are creating a listing. Selecting relevant groups will bring your listing to a very targeted audience. Joining local groups will allow more people in your area to see your listing. The more people who see your listing, the more likely you are to sell it quickly.

CHAPTER 6

TAKING GREAT PHOTOS

Photos are the first thing people notice when they look at Marketplace listings, so you want them to look as good as possible. The majority of buyers say that photos are more important than the descriptions. I think they are equally important, but it is the photos that will usually catch a buyer's attention when they are scrolling through Marketplace.

Taking high quality photos is easy with today's smartphones. Follow the tips below to improve the quality of your photos.

Once you have taken the photos, it is easy to upload them to Marketplace. People like to see as many photos as possible, so go ahead and take a lot. Marketplace allows you to use up to ten photos in each listing.

Photography Tips

The best lighting for photos is natural lighting. Take your photos outside if possible or near a window. Check your photos as you are taking them to make sure there aren't shadows in them.

Make sure your photos are not blurry. If you have a shaky hand and can't hold your phone still, then consider attaching it to a tripod. Depending on the size of the item you are photographing, you can use either a desktop tripod or a full size one. Tripods are relatively inexpensive and would make a useful addition to your business.

Clean your camera lens on your phone. If you take some photos and notice that they just don't look that great, it could be that your camera lens on your phone is dirty. Oftentimes it will have fingerprint smudges on it that can affect photo quality. It can also get dust or other debris on it.

To clean your camera lens, breathe on it gently to get a little moisture on it. Then wipe it with a microfiber cloth. That's it. If your pictures still aren't clear, try turning off your phone and restarting it.

Get rid of as much background clutter as possible. Take a photo and look at it closely. Do you see a pile of dirty laundry or a bag of dog food in the background? Clean up the area where you are going to take photos. If the background looks bad, then potential buyers will question the quality of the item you are selling. You can buy a white, three-sided project board at most dollar stores and use it as a background if you don't have a good place in your home to take photos.

Take photos from multiple angles. Zoom in and show details. Does that antique chair you are trying to sell have some incredible carvings on it? Get close-ups of those details to show to potential buyers. Selling a rare set of Haviland Limoges china? Flip it over and show the maker's mark on the back. Buyers want to see as many details as possible before they make the commitment to buy your item.

What if what you are selling has flaws or imperfections? As long as you disclose that information in your description and show photos of the damaged areas, then you have covered your bases. As we all know, imperfections can reduce the value of antiques, but the fact that you openly shared that information greatly increases your credibility and shows that you are an honest seller. As I mentioned in Chapter 2, there is a market for items that are not perfect. Buyers just need to know this information before you agree on a price and meet with them.

Since Marketplace allows you to use up to ten photos, you should try to use all ten of the available spots. By the time you take photos of each item and include close-ups, different angles, maker's marks, and imperfections, it is easy to come up with ten photos.

Editing Your Photos

Before you upload your photos to your listing, take a close look at each of them, keeping the tips listed above in mind. You may need to crop them to remove extraneous items in the background and retake photos that are blurry or have bad lighting. If your photos are too dark, then you should try photographing them outdoors or use better lighting indoors. Try to do most of your editing before you upload the photos to Marketplace. Your phone typically offers better editing tools than those available through Marketplace.

Once you have uploaded your photos, preview how they look. You may still need to do some fine tuning. Marketplace gives you the option of editing the photos. You might need to crop them in order for them to look their best in the listing photos.

When you are choosing photos from your phone to use in your listing, select them in the order that you want them to appear. Generally, your first photo should be one that shows the entire item. However, if there is a detail that makes your item unique and more desirable then start with that photo.

You cannot change the order once you have added them to your listing. If you do want to change the order, you will have to delete all of the photos and then add them back in the order in which you want them to appear.

Photo Editing Tools

There are numerous photo editing apps that you can use to improve the quality of your photos. Your phone has some tools included on it and you should start with those, but if you really want to improve the quality of your listing photos then try out some of the photo apps.

Go to the app store on your phone and search for photo editor. You will see that there are many photo editing tools to choose from. One of the ones that I have found to be very useful is PicCollage.

I have recently started using PicCollage to create at least one of the photos for each of my listings. PicCollage allows you to create photo collages using simple grids that are part of the app. If you have several items that you are including as part of a single listing or if there are a couple of things that you really want to emphasize in a listing, this tool lets you display them in one photo. Sometimes I like to create a collage to use as my first photo so that I can share as much visual information as possible since the first photo is the one that people use to decide whether or not they are going to click on my listing.

Do Not Use Stock Photos or Someone Else's Photos

While it might be tempting, resist the urge to use stock photos or someone else's photos. Stock photos may look great, but they can be misleading to buyers because they might not accurately represent the item you have for sale. This is also true for random photos that you find on the internet of items similar to yours. For example, WorthPoint is an excellent tool for researching sold prices on antiques and you can often find an item that is very similar to yours on their site. Their photos might look a lot better than any of the photos you have taken. The person who took the WorthPoint photos might be a better photographer than you are or have access to better lighting and equipment, and as a result, have beautiful photos of an item that is very similar to yours. It may be tempting to take a screen shot of their photo and use it in your listing. Don't do it.

There are several reasons why you shouldn't use someone else's photos. First, they may not accurately reflect the item you are trying to sell. Perhaps the color or style is slightly different or yours was made in a different dye lot. Second, some potential buyers might perceive your listing to be fraudulent because the photos you are using were not taken by you and are not of the specific item you have for sale. They may think you are being dishonest and are hiding what your item actually looks like. Third, if there are any flaws in your item, they obviously won't show up in someone else's photos. Sometimes people only look at the photos and not the description. If they look at someone else's photos, they will expect your item to look exactly like the one in the photo. Yes, it is tempting to use those perfect photos, but just don't do it.

Just Take the Photos

Take the best photos that you can, but don't stress about it too much. You want your photos to be clear, crisp, flattering, etc., but the most important thing is that you just take the photos and get the items listed. Don't hold off listing something because you think your photos aren't good enough or professional enough. They are. They may not be perfect, but they are good enough for a Marketplace listing and they will keep getting better the more you list. Remember, buyers can request more photos if there is a specific detail they want to see on your item, so you can always take more photos and share them with potential buyers after you create your listing.

CHAPTER 7

PROMOTING YOUR LISTING

You've taken photos, created your listing, and clicked Publish. What else can you do to make the sale? Here are a few extra things that you should do to enhance your listings.

List in Groups

How to select and join groups is covered in Chapter 5. Promoting and sharing your listings with different groups is one of the best ways to put your items in front of potential buyers. While technically not Marketplace, you can also list your items in groups that you have joined. Just check the group rules first. Some encourage buying and selling and some are strictly for discussing and sharing photos and information about your antiques. Follow their rules. They may let you break their rules once but if you do it again, they will often kick you out and block you from joining again. It is kind of harsh, but it keeps them focused and true to their stated purpose.

Renew Your Listings

If you list an item and it hasn't sold within a week, Marketplace gives you the option of renewing the listing. Renewing the listing moves it up in Marketplace so that it is more likely to get more views.

Sometimes Marketplace will send you a message asking if you have sold an item. If you answer no, then it will offer to relist an item for you. It doesn't do this with every listing, so if you don't get a message from Marketplace then you can follow the steps below to renew a listing.

To renew a listing:

1. Go to Marketplace.

2. Click on the person icon in the top left corner.

3. Click on Your Listings.

4. Click on the item you want to renew. You must wait at least seven days before you can renew a listing.

5. Click Renew Post.

You can renew every seven days (maximum of five times per listing). If Renew Listing is not available as an option, it has either not been seven days since you last renewed it, or you have already renewed it five times and it cannot be renewed again. If it has already been renewed five times and you still haven't sold it, consider deleting the current listing and create a new listing with new photos.

Paid Promotions / Boost Listing

If you are in a hurry to sell your item, you can consider using paid promotions, i.e., boosting your listing. Personally, I don't spend money selling on Marketplace, so I have not tried this option. I like that I can list and sell for free, so I don't use boost my listings. However, it is definitely something you can experiment with and see if it works for you. Obviously since there are expenses involved, then you will need to do your research to determine how much you want to spend. You wouldn't want to spend your time and money promoting a low-priced item, but you might want to on a very expensive one. I suggest starting with a small amount of money and see how it goes.

According to Marketplace, boosting a listing increases the number of people who see a listing and may help you sell your item faster. Boosting a listing turns it into a Facebook ad that will appear in multiple places including Facebook's news feed.

Recently I listed a set of mid-century modern bookends for sale on Marketplace. The listing ran for a few days but still had not sold. At this point, Marketplace suggested that I boost my listing. According to Marketplace, spending three dollars to boost the listing for this specific item would enable me to reach 196 more people.

According to their statistics, sellers that boost their items:

- Get 2.5 times more listing views.

- Connect with 57 percent more potential buyers.

- Receive messages 1.5 times faster.

To boost your listing:

1. Open the item that you have listed on Marketplace.

2. Click Boost Listing.

3. Set your maximum budget.

4. Select how long you want your ad to run.

5. Select a payment method.

6. Click Boost Listing.

7. Your boosted listing will be promoted in the Facebook news feed and in Marketplace.

I sold those bookends a couple of weeks later without boosting the listing. If you have the time, then your patience will usually pay off, but if you are in a hurry then you might consider paying to boost your listing.

Tip: Occasionally Marketplace will offer to promote your item for free. This is their way of introducing you to this type of paid promotion. Definitely give it a try if they are offering a free promotion.

CHAPTER 8

WHAT TO DO IF YOUR ITEM ISN'T SELLING

D on't you love it when you list something, and you immediately start getting messages about it? Your phone sends you multiple notifications, you make an appointment, and then you sell your item the same day.

Sometimes though, that just doesn't happen. Not only do you not receive any messages, but your listing doesn't even get any views. You immediately start to wonder what is going on. There are a number of factors that can come into play when a listing doesn't sell, but you can easily go in and make changes to your listing and hopefully sell your item quickly.

Consider these Changes

If you feel like your item hasn't sold in a reasonable amount of time, then it is time to look for ways to make your listing more appealing. Here are some ideas that should help.

1. Lower the price. One of the best ways to stir up new interest in your listing is to go ahead and start lowering the price. It doesn't have to be a huge reduction. Consider reducing the price by five or ten percent. As you consider how much you might need to lower your price, do your research and see what other similar items are selling for. Perhaps Marketplace has suddenly become flooded with items similar to yours, or possibly other sellers have comparable items priced much lower than yours. Check out the competition and make sure your price is in line with what others are asking. Look at the prices on eBay and Etsy too. Customers will often look there and expect Marketplace listings to have lower prices.

   Marketplace lets users know if you have lowered your price on an item. If you have lowered the price, potential customers will see the original price with a line drawn through it and the new lower price next to it. If it is a listing that the customer has looked at before and saved, Marketplace will notify them that you have lowered the price. This is a great feature and an easy way to get your item in front of interested customers. Seeing the lower price often motivates buyers to purchase an item.

2. Is your item seasonal? Vintage Christmas decorations definitely sell better from late October through December. If your item is seasonal, consider removing your listing for now and relisting it during the appropriate season.

3. How do your pictures look? Are they appealing? Are they blurry? Does your item look desirable or just old? Did you take the photos in your garage with random items in the background and poor lighting, or did you take the time to stage it so that it looks its best? If your photos are not that good, consider taking new photos and replacing the existing ones.

4. Is your item clean? If your item is covered in dust, rust, or dirt, then it may look unappealing to buyers. You might be okay with an old gasoline sign that has some rust around the edges, but you don't want one covered in dirt or spider webs. Clean it up, take new pictures, and relist your item.

5. Reread your description and compare it to other similar listings. Make sure you are including the same type of information that other sellers have included in their listings. Add any details that you may have left out.

6. Start over. If the suggestions above don't work, consider creating a new listing and deleting the old one. This will move the item up in searches and may put it in front of someone who has just started searching for an item like yours. Reword the title and description and take new photos of your item to include in the listing. At the beginning of this chapter, I mentioned lowering your price. If you are creating a new listing for an item that hasn't sold, you might want to consider raising the price. Some customers

are suspicious of items if they think the price is too low. Rather than thinking they are getting a bargain, they wonder what is wrong with it.

Tip: Cleaning your items is great but you might not want to go overboard with it. For example, dealers have been debating for years over whether it is better to polish antique silver or sell it with a nicely aged patina. I go back and forth on this one because both looks can be beautiful. I tend to not polish it simply because a buyer can purchase your silver and polish it themselves to make it look shiny and new, but they can't remove the polish and bring back that tarnished look. In this case, I prefer to leave the decision (and the work) up to the buyer. The same is true for wooden pieces. You can't replicate the patina that comes from an item being very old. You don't want to sand off that patina and stain it just to cover up a few scuffs or scratches. In doing so, you can reduce the value of an item.

CHAPTER 9

SAFETY

When you first start selling your items on Marketplace, safety can be an overwhelming concern. While safety is something you always need to be aware of, as you complete more and more transactions, you will quickly learn the safest ways to handle your transactions and you will become more comfortable with the process. I would say two of the most important safety-related things to do are: use common sense and pay attention to your surroundings. And one more thing: follow your instincts. Most transactions are relatively simple, but if you don't have a good feeling about the person you are scheduled to meet, then just don't do it. It is not worth risking your safety.

The following guidelines will help make the experience safer and should help ease your concerns. Some of the suggestions mentioned below are common sense and they may actually be things that you already do.

Update Your Personal Page

Both buyers and sellers need to take precautions when using Marketplace. Just as you will check out a potential buyer's Facebook profile, they will do the same with you. Before you create a Marketplace listing, check your personal profile to see what information is public and make any necessary adjustments. You may want to remove some personal information that you wouldn't want buyers to know about such as your phone number or your employer's name or location. Also, you may want to make your account private. If you do this, the buyer can see a few details about you, but most things are private and reserved only for your actual Facebook friends.

You should make these changes to your Facebook account before you create any listings.

Check Out the Buyer's Facebook Page

Let's say you've been in contact with a potential buyer, and you are ready to make a deal. Well, hold on. Don't immediately set up a time. Take a few minutes to look at their Facebook page. Look on their personal page and do your own "background check."

Check to see if you have any mutual friends. Search to see if there is more than one account with their name and photo. This is a red flag. See if their account appears to be a new one or if they only have a few friends. If it is a new account and they don't have many friends, that could be a sign that it is not a legitimate account. It is definitely a sign that you should proceed with caution.

Let Someone Know Where You Are

Before you leave to meet your customer, let a friend or family member know what you are doing, where you are meeting, and the time you are meeting. If both parties show up on time, then the transaction normally only takes a few minutes. If either of you is running late, then let your friend know.

If you are still uncomfortable, you could even ask your friend to call or text you if they haven't heard from you by a designated time. After you have completed the transaction, let your friend know (Don't forget this step.) that the transaction was successful and that you have left the meeting location.

Meet in a Public Place

Many local police stations have designated areas in their parking lots for online sellers. This is a great option, especially for new sellers who might be nervous about meeting customers.

I do most of my transactions at a local grocery store parking lot that is usually full of customers. I try to get there first and park in an open part of the parking lot that has a lot of visibility. I also try to make sure there are empty parking spaces on either side of me. I check out my surroundings, looking for anyone or anything that might seem suspicious. Before I leave to meet a customer, we usually let each other know what type and color vehicle we are driving. If you aren't sure if you recognize a customer, then text them before you get out of your car to confirm their identity. Simply say something as simple as, "I am here in the third row towards the back of the parking lot." That will give them some reassurance too, knowing that they are about to approach the correct person.

I almost never meet anyone after dark. I'm just not comfortable with that.

When You Have to Meet at Your Home

If you are selling a large piece of furniture, then you will probably want the customer to come to your house to pick it up. You won't want to risk damaging it by loading it into your vehicle yourself to take it to a meeting place. Also (and it happens sometimes but not too often) if the buyer doesn't show up, you will have to take it home and unload it.

Try to have someone at home with you if you are having a customer meet you at your home, especially if they will need to actually come into your home to pick up the item. It is simply too risky to have a stranger come into your house with no one else there. There is also a good chance that they will bring someone with them because they may have the same safety concerns that you have, and they may need to bring someone to help them move the furniture.

Porch Pick Up

Porch pickups are a popular option for many people, and it is exactly what it sounds like. You place the item on your porch and the customer comes to your house, pays, and then picks it up. Some people prefer this option because you can do it without any physical contact. You don't even have to be home.

Of course, if you choose this option, then your buyer will obviously need to know where you live. I rarely use porch pickups, but many people prefer this option. If you do decide to use porch pickups and you are going to be at home for the pickup, I recommend having someone at home with you during the agreed upon time, or if you won't be home, be sure and message the seller to let them know exactly where you will place the item they are purchasing. If you are going to be at home for a porch pickup, it is up to you to decide whether or not you will actually go outside and meet your buyer in person. Some people just don't like the idea of having someone come to their home when they are not there.

When scheduling the pickup, make it clear to your buyer where you want them to leave their money (such as under your doormat). If you prefer, you can have them pay you electronically through PayPal or Venmo or whichever form of electronic payment that you prefer.

Oftentimes, people use porch pickups for inexpensive items. I wouldn't use it for expensive items, especially if you are worried that someone might drive by and steal the item from your porch.

Another reason many sellers prefer porch pickups is because they don't always have time to meet a buyer. If you have a busy schedule, it may be tough to find a time that works for both you and the buyer.

Use Messenger to Communicate with Customers

Make sure you do all your communication through the Facebook Messenger app. You don't want to give out your personal information (phone number, address, email) to everyone who might be viewing your listing. When you come to a purchase agreement with your customer, then you can give them your phone number if you like, or you can continue to communicate exclusively through Messenger. The Messenger app links your conversations to your listings and makes it easy to keep up with your listing communications.

Have Someone Go with You

As I mentioned earlier, when I first started selling on Marketplace I would either have my husband meet my customer or at least go with me. I don't do that anymore, unless we just already happen to be going somewhere together at the time I am meeting a customer. Plenty of people do bring someone with them. For me it is about fifty-fifty. About half of my customers bring someone with them to purchase an item. You might want to do this in the beginning if meeting customers by yourself makes you nervous and then you can eventually meet customers by yourself when you are more comfortable with the process.

Have Someone on the Phone with You

Now I don't do this, but if it makes you feel more comfortable, then have someone stay on the phone with you during the transaction. You don't even have to pull out your phone. You can simply keep it in your pocket while on call with a friend (Make sure you have your phone's speaker turned on.). That way, if something goes wrong, you will have someone who can hear your conversation and take action if necessary. Again, I don't do this and I don't think it is necessary, but it may be something you want to do until you feel more comfortable with meeting customers. I have noticed that some of my customers do this.

Just Say No if You Aren't Comfortable

If something that the buyer says during your text messages or phone conversations makes you uncomfortable then just say no. Sometimes they can be too pushy or sometimes they say something that sounds strange or just doesn't sound right. It's your call. You can always find another buyer.

Tell them that the item is no longer available. You can even block them so that they can no longer see any of your posts or your personal Facebook page. If someone is being difficult or makes you uncomfortable in any way, then just say no and move on. It is important to go with your gut feeling on this. No sale is worth putting yourself at risk.

It's Going to be Okay

With all that I have said regarding safety, I think it is going to be okay. I feel like I have made this whole experience sound very scary and I realize that it can be to some people when starting out. It is important to take precautions, pay attention to your surroundings, and not take any chances. However, I think that once you start selling on Marketplace and become more comfortable with the process, you will see that the precautions I have covered are very common-sense things and some of them are things that you already do. You probably do them without even thinking about it.

The more you sell, the more comfortable you will become with the process. Just be careful and keep these tips in mind. They will eventually become second nature.

CHAPTER 10

PRICING

Excellent photography, detailed descriptions, and rare items are great, they really are, but people are looking for deals. You probably already know this from selling in your other venues and from shopping for yourself. Marketplace buyers usually expect a little better deal than what you might get for something in your booth or on Etsy or eBay. While you may hesitate to offer a lower price, remember, that as long as you are selling locally and not shipping your item, you will have absolutely no overhead costs with Marketplace. Unlike an antique booth with monthly rental fees and commissions or Etsy and eBay with listing fees, commissions, PayPal fees and shipping costs, you have none of that with Marketplace. With that in mind, you can consider offering a lower price than what you would charge at those other places.

Research Your Competition

To determine what your item is worth, you will need to do some research. Look on Etsy and eBay to see what your item is selling for there. With Etsy, you can only see the listing prices. They don't share any sold prices. With eBay however, you can look at sold listings and find the price that an item actually sold for. To do this, click on the Advanced Search option next to the main Search button. Enter the name of your item in the search box then scroll down and click Sold Listings, and then Search. This will give you a list of what similar items have sold for over the past few months.

You also need to look and see what the item is selling for on Marketplace. Simply search for your item to see other sellers' prices. Be sure and conduct multiple searches if your item might be called different things. For example, a Victorian couch might also be called a sofa, davenport, or settee. Also search Facebook selling groups to see how much items are selling for in those groups.

When comparing your item to what others have listed, make sure that in addition to comparing price, that you also compare the condition of the item. Perhaps your piece is in mint or near-mint condition and that would make it worth significantly more than a similar item that has some damage or wear.

How Quickly Do You Need to Make a Sale?

Once you have done your research, it is time to decide on a price. If you are in a hurry to make a sale, say for example, that you are closing your antique booth or you need to empty a storage unit by the end of the month and you need to quickly sell your merchandise, then you will need to take that into consideration when determining price. If that is the case, I would look at what others on Marketplace are listing their items for and price yours at five to ten percent less. If you aren't in a hurry to make a sale, then you could list it at the same price or slightly more than your competition.

How Rare is It?

If your item is rare and you are having a hard time finding comparables on Marketplace, then go with a higher price. Just remember you may not be as likely to find a buyer in your particular market. For rare items, you may have to go to a larger venue such as Etsy or eBay. It is worth a shot though. Try listing it for a few weeks and see if you get any takers.

Price to Sell

A mistake that many sellers make is pricing their item for more than it is worth. Face it; we all know that the price of antiques has gone down over the past ten to twenty years. If you are trying to sell an antique desk that you paid two thousand dollars for in 1992 for that same price, then you probably aren't going to get much interest. Even something that you purchased just five or ten years ago will have potentially gone down in value too. This isn't always easy to accept, especially if you bought the item as an investment. However, if you want to sell it in today's market, then you have to sell it for what it is currently worth. Do your research and find out the current prices of similar items.

While some items have gone down in value, others have seen their values increase. As recently as ten to fifteen years ago, people were practically giving away mid-century modern pieces. These pieces have gone up significantly in value and are very popular now. Some vintage items from the 1980s and 1990s have also become quite popular.

If you really want your item to stand out and sell more quickly, you should think about pricing it lower than the prices of your competitors. It doesn't have to be a lot lower. Consider starting out at five percent lower than your competition. This may be just enough to attract buyers to check out and hopefully buy your item instead of one of the others listed on Marketplace.

You never know what your buyer's situation may be. Some people are serious researchers and will look at all the available pieces and text you lots of questions. They aren't in any rush and want to carefully evaluate all options before making a decision. Others might be in a hurry to make a purchase (perhaps they are shopping for a gift) and want to buy the first item that meets their criteria. You will have to decide whether you want to wait for the best price or sell it more quickly for a lower price.

Does it Stand Out from the Competition?

After researching similar items on Marketplace, try to think of ways to make your item stand out. Make sure you use as many photos as possible and that they are of excellent quality. Include photos that show the item in use. If your price is higher than that of your competitors, then you will want to visually attract buyers and show why your item is worth more.

If there is something that makes your item unique, be sure and include that information in the title and in the first sentence of your description. You can include descriptive words such as "rare" and "hard to find" if those terms accurately describe your item. You want to remember that buyers don't always read the entire description, so you need to have the most important information in the first couple of sentences. You want the buyers to focus on your listing over all the others. If you are selling an antique cast iron bathtub that is 82 inches long and all the other ones are only 77 inches long, then that information needs to be included in your title and at the beginning of your description. It should also be reflected in your price. Explain why this increases the value, and then list it at a higher price. For something like this you should include the actual measurement and also use terms such as extra-long or oversized.

If you are offering a more appealing product than your competitors, then there is a good chance that you can get a higher price than them. Try to think of things that make your product better than the competition and then share that information with potential buyers. This should help you sell it for a higher price.

Negotiating

Negotiating is a very important part of the sales process. You are going to have to negotiate most of the time with Marketplace buyers. As a general rule, many of them just love to haggle. Not only should you expect the haggling, you have got to have a thick skin. You can't get offended or angered by offers. It is just part of the process. Your price should be a little bit higher than what you are willing to accept. This will leave you room for negotiating and leave the buyers feeling accomplished for getting your item at a lower price.

However, if you are not willing to come down on your price then you should state that in your listing. Simply state that the price is firm or non-negotiable. I usually leave some wiggle room in prices so that I can negotiate with the buyer. However, I have had a few items that I priced competitively, and I simply told the buyer that the price was fair when they asked for a discount. Most of the buyers told me that they agreed that my price was fair, they just wanted to see if I would go any lower!

If you have just recently lowered your price, you can tell potential buyers that you have just lowered the price on your listing and you are not willing to go any lower on the price at this time.

Sometimes buyers will come in with lowball offers. I have had people offer me fifty percent or less of what I was asking for an item. While it would have been easy to be annoyed or offended by offers like that, you can't let it bother you. You might even be inclined to just tell them no. Don't do that though. Lowball offers just come with the territory. It is just how some people work.

Counter their offer with one slightly higher than the lowest amount you are willing to take for your item. For example, if you have a one-hundred-dollar item and the absolute lowest price you will accept for it is eighty dollars, then counter their offer with ninety dollars. This will give some room to have a little more back and forth with the buyer.

However, if it is the first day you have something listed, it is perfectly acceptable to tell your customer that you just listed it and you want to see if you get a better offer. While you should never be rude to a customer, you can politely tell them that their offer is too low and that you cannot accept it at this time.

Sometimes customers immediately recognize a good deal or they find something that they really want, and they don't even discuss price. They are perfectly happy to pay full price.

It is always such a nice experience when this happens. Don't second guess yourself and wonder if you priced it too low. Just be glad that you were able to sell it quickly for the price that you wanted. As antique dealers, we are always looking for the best deals and often have to negotiate to get those deals, but I think we have all dealt with customers who simply want what they want and don't care about the price.

Speaking of which, if you are more interested in selling something quickly than getting top dollar for it, then you can include OBO in your listing which stands for Or Best Offer. You are more likely to get lower offers when you use OBO, but you are still in control, and you can decide how low you are willing to go.

Handling Multiple Offers

If you have just recently listed something for sale and several offers start coming in at the same time, just take a deep breath. You don't have to immediately decide which offer you are going to accept. If you are not satisfied with one offer but you are hesitant to turn it down because you are not sure if you will receive other offers, just tell the buyer that you are considering all offers at that time and you will let them know. Sometimes telling the buyer this will motivate them to go ahead and purchase your item at your original price. You do run the risk of them purchasing a similar item from another seller or of them losing interest, but it may be worth the wait if you aren't in a rush and you are selling a popular or hard-to-find item.

CHAPTER 11

WRITING GREAT DESCRIPTIONS

Be Thorough

It is important to provide thorough descriptions. While you don't want your listing to get too wordy and cause potential buyers to lose interest, you need to provide enough information to help buyers decide that they want to purchase your item.

Detailed descriptions can save you time in the long run. If you include as many details as possible in your description, then you greatly reduce the amount of back-and-forth texting with buyers asking for those details. Texting back and forth with your customers might not sound like a big deal, but if you are having text conversations with several people at once, it can start to feel overwhelming and it can be very time consuming. You can also get messages mixed up and accidentally send messages to the wrong person. I have done this before and it can take additional time as you try to sort out your conversations and make sure everyone has the information that goes with the item that they are interested in.

In addition, detailed descriptions reduce the likelihood that a customer will be disappointed or surprised when they finally meet with you in person. You have given them all of the information they need to decide if your item is right for them. Thorough descriptions also help demonstrate that you are an honest, up-front seller who isn't trying to hide anything.

You need to be prepared to repeat information once you start communicating with customers. Even though you may include every possible detail that you can think of in your description, there are some people who do not read the descriptions that closely or they only read the first couple of lines of your description. Some people don't even read the entire title if it is a long one. You need to have a thorough description but also be prepared for the occasional customer who does not read it. You've got to try to not be annoyed with customers who ask questions about something that is already in the description. Some people just don't pay attention to the details.

Remember that you and the buyer will both be taking the time to meet up with each other, whether at your house or at a designated location, and you don't want them to be disappointed in the item and then change their mind once they see it. It will end up being a waste of time for both of you. Also, if you meet with a potential buyer and they are disappointed and don't go through with the purchase, then logically you will think to sell it to the next person who showed interest in it (if you have a back-up buyer). The risk in this is that the second buyer may have already found something similar to buy from another seller or may have lost interest in the item and then you will be out of luck. You want your buyer to be well informed before you meet so that they will be satisfied and go through with the purchase when you finally meet in person.

What to Include in a Listing

Try to think of everything you would want to know about the type of item you are listing. With antiques, age, condition, and maker's marks are a few things that come to mind. Obviously, the type of information included will differ depending on what you are listing. Think of the small details that would make it most appealing to you and make sure you include that information.

Some of the things you want to be sure and include in your descriptions are:

- Color: Sometimes colors do not display correctly on the screen. It may be the buyer's phone or computer screen, or it might be the quality of the photo you posted. Providing the color in the description can help the buyer decide on your item.

- Size: measurements.

- Any imperfections or damage: Even if the imperfections are barely noticeable, go ahead and disclose them and include photos if possible. This will prevent your customer from being disappointed if they notice damage when you meet in person.

- Maker's marks: You should include information on all maker's marks and include photos of the marks. However, if the item does not have a maker's mark that is okay too. Sometimes maker's marks are etched onto an item and they are difficult to photograph. If this is the case, then you will need to provide a written description as best you can.

- Provenance: If you have any documents or photos that show the history of your item, be sure to include them in your description. Sometimes pieces of antique artwork will have handwritten notes on the back. Include photos and explain the provenance if you have it.

- Age: This may require some research, as is often the case with antiques, but do your best to identify and include the age of the object.

- Unique features: What makes the item different from other similar pieces? Is it a unique color or finish? Does it have extra features not normally associated with that item? Include what makes it unique because it may also increase its value or at least its desirability.

- If it goes by multiple names: People will search for an item based on what they call that item. If you have an antique tole tray, be sure to also identify it as a metal tray, painted tray, decorative tray, etc. A secretary may also be called a desk, china cabinet, or bookcase. Try to think of all the possible names for an item so your customer will be more likely to find it when they do a search.

- What it is made of: Be sure to include all materials that an item may be made of, especially if it may not be clear in the photos. Some vintage plastic pieces were designed to look like wood. If an item is solid wood then say so, but also let the customer know if it is a laminate or made from some other material.

Include Measurements

Include measurements of the item. You will need to include the length, width, and height. Sometimes it helps if you include something in your photos that can be used to give customers an idea of scale. For example, sometimes I will take a picture of an item that I am listing next to a Coke can to help the buyer visualize the size/scale of the item. If it is a piece of jewelry, I might photograph it next to a quarter.

If your listing is for a piece of furniture, your buyer will need to know if it is going to fit in the space they have in mind for it. They will also need to know if it is going to fit in their vehicle or if they might need to bring a larger vehicle to pick it up.

Measurements are important for smaller items too. If it is a painting, then the buyer will want to know if it will fit in their designated spot. If they are trying to add pieces to their china pattern, they will want to know if the piece you are selling is the size of a fruit bowl or a butter pat. The larger size of a book might be worth significantly more than a smaller size (or vice versa).

Include Unique Features

Is there something unique about the piece you are selling? Is your book signed by the author or is it a first edition? Does your pottery have a unique glazing feature? Is there a misprint on your stamp or coin? Is your sculpture a one-of-a-kind piece by a famous designer/artist? Describe any feature that makes your item stand out from others. Research to see if the type of unique property your item has is more likely to increase or decrease its value.

Describe Imperfections

As you know, any damage, even the tiniest chip or crack, can greatly reduce the value of an antique. A one-hundred-dollar vase may only be worth twenty to thirty dollars if it is cracked or chipped, even if the damage is not that noticeable.

However, there is a market for items with minor damage. If, for example, your buyer collects McCoy pottery and you are offering a rare red poppy vase that they have wanted for years, then that particular collector might be willing to pay more for it for their personal collection, even with minor damage, than someone who is buying it as an investment to resell. They will buy it because they realize the scarcity of the item and they just want to add it to their collection, damaged or not. They are buying it for the enjoyment of having that piece as part of their collection and aren't as concerned about it being perfect.

If the item you are selling does have imperfections, make sure you include clear pictures of the affected areas. Include something in the photo that will give the buyer an idea of the size of the damaged area. For example, you might take a picture of it with a pencil tip pointing to the damage so they can have a better idea of the extent of the damage.

If I have a piece that has a tiny chip that is so small that it just doesn't show up in a photograph, I will take a picture of it anyway and then say that it is very hard to see but you can feel it. You can also use the photo editing feature on your phone to circle or point to the damaged area. You can describe the damage as something that you might notice when you rub your finger around the rim of a glass that has a small nick, not noticeable when you look at it, but you can feel it when you touch it.

Include History/Provenance if You Have It

Knowing the exact history of an item you have for sale can add to its value. It definitely makes it more interesting. An item's provenance (its history of ownership) can be demonstrated in a number of ways. Providing thorough documentation of provenance helps confirm an item's authenticity. One of the simplest ways to demonstrate provenance is with a picture of the antique with its original owner in its original or early location. If the item's owner was famous and you have a photo of it with the owner, then that can increase the value even more. Other methods of demonstrating provenance include providing original receipts, handwritten notes or inscriptions, and certificates of authenticity.

If you have an antique and you can show that through its provenance that it is worth a lot of money, you may want to rethink selling it on Marketplace. It might be better suited to a high-end website such as Chairish or 1stdibs.

Proofread for Grammatical Errors

You've got great pictures. You've written a thorough description. It is time to click Publish, right? Wrong. Taking the time to proofread your titles and descriptions can really make a difference. You might catch a mistake that could end up costing you a lot of money. You wouldn't want to accidentally publish a listing for 25 dollars when you actually planned on listing it for 250 dollars.

Carefully reviewing your listing before you publish it shows that you care that it is the best that it can be, and subconsciously, buyers translate a quality listing with a quality product. If you don't take time to review your content and make it error free, then in their mind they begin to question not only the quality of the item you are selling, but also the honesty and accuracy of your description.

You need to proofread for grammatical mistakes and misspelled words. If your spelling is too far off, there is always a chance that the potential buyer will not be able to find your listing because the search term they enter is different from the misspelled word in your description.

You also need to proofread for accuracy. Make sure you didn't accidentally say that the antique book you are listing was published in 1796 when it was actually published in 1897 or that the highboy is 47 inches tall when it is actually 74 inches tall. Double check that your description is 100 percent accurate. It will save both you and the buyer from headaches and it will enhance your reputation.

CHAPTER 12

Shipping

Marketplace gives you the option of listing your items with local pickup, shipping, or offering both options. As I have already mentioned, I use Marketplace for local transactions only. Many of the items that I sell on Marketplace would be challenging to ship. For example, I often sell complete sets of antique china/dishes on Marketplace. The shipping materials needed to securely wrap a fifty or sixty piece set of china would be quite expensive and still would not guarantee a safe delivery. I think most of us have seen videos of delivery drivers carelessly throwing packages onto their customers' porches. I have had china pieces arrive shattered even though they were carefully wrapped.

Because some of the things that I sell are often fragile and rare, I prefer to sell them locally and avoid the risk of them being damaged during shipping. While I might be able to sell something for a higher price on Etsy or eBay, sometimes it isn't worth the hassle and the risk involved with shipping. Just as with anything you choose to sell, you will need to weigh the pros and cons, and decide what will work best for you.

Furniture is another type of item that can be difficult to ship. Many pieces are large and heavy and can be quite expensive to ship.

Setting up Shipping

If you do decide to ship the items that you are selling, it is a simple process. First though you have to make sure that Marketplace will allow you to ship. You may not be able to ship items when you first start using Markeplace. Facebook puts shipping restrictions on new accounts. These restrictions are meant to protect buyers.

If you decide you want to ship items through Marketplace and you have been cleared to do so, click on Shipping when you are creating your listing and follow the instructions. You will have three business days to ship your item.

Selling Fee

At this time, Facebook charges a five percent selling fee for items sold with shipping. The fee charged is based on the total combined price of the item, shipping, and taxes. When you factor in the cost of shipping supplies and selling fees, it can really add up.

Receiving Payment

Once you have shipped your item and entered the tracking information, Facebook will begin processing your payment. You will receive payment for the items you sold in approximately fifteen to twenty days after you have shipped your item.

CHAPTER 13

WHEN TO LIST AN ITEM FOR SALE

Choosing the best time to list an item for sale is an important consideration. While it might be tempting to list an item whenever it is convenient for you or right after you purchase it, you might want to rethink that strategy.

List Your Items on Fridays and Saturdays

Most sales on Marketplace take place on the weekends. I recommend listing items on Friday afternoons or Saturday mornings. While there isn't a way for you to guarantee placement, by following this strategy, your listing is more likely to show up near the top of a buyer's search results if they start looking at listings on the weekends.

Another Reason to List on Fridays or Saturdays

Antique stores are busiest on weekends and most estate sale companies hold their sales on weekends too. If a potential customer sees something they like at an antique store, but they want to compare prices or they just missed out on something that they saw on an estate sale listing, Marketplace is the next logical place to do their shopping/comparisons. Marketplace displays newly listed items closer to the top of their search result list. By listing your items on Friday evenings or Saturday mornings, your item will be well positioned near or at the top of a potential buyer's search results.

Renewing Your Listings

I discussed the importance of renewing your listings in Chapter 7 and explained how to do it. Sometimes I forget to renew my listings at the end of the seven-day period. Oftentimes, but not always, Facebook will ask me if my item has sold and remind me to renew the listing. These reminders pop up randomly in Facebook Messenger throughout the week. Although it is easier to just immediately renew the listing when you get one of these reminders, I recommend that you wait and renew them on the weekend so that your listing has the best chance of being seen by the most potential customers.

CHAPTER 14

COMMUNICATING WITH BUYERS

After you have created your listing and published it, it is time to make your first sale. The next step in this process is essential to successfully completing your sale: communicating effectively with potential buyers.

The buyer has two ways that they can communicate with you on Marketplace. They can either click the Is this Available button to check on an item's availability or they can select the Message button to access Facebook Messenger and send a private message to you.

Is this Available?

The easiest way for a buyer to communicate with you is by clicking the Is this Available button. It requires the least amount of effort from the buyer. Once you receive a message through this feature, you can simply respond to this message with a single word "Yes" to the buyer, but I don't recommend that.

Even though they haven't requested more information, this is your chance to start promoting/selling your item. Never just say yes. Add a statement such as:

- Yes, would you like to meet and purchase it today?

- Yes, can I answer any other questions about it?

- Yes, but there are three (or however many there are) other people already interested in it. Would you like to meet to purchase it now?

- Yes, but I have a pending offer. I can let you know if that does not work out. This may motivate them to act more quickly.

- Yes, here is something unique about my item that differentiates it from other listings.

It is important to keep the conversation going. Just saying yes may come across as rude or abrupt to some people, or possibly give the impression that you are not that motivated to make a sale. Try to engage your customer. It can help close the deal.

Facebook Messenger

Many customers will contact you through Facebook Messenger. This is an easy and private way to communicate with your customers and a lot of customers will use Messenger if they have questions that they want to ask you about the item that you are selling. Messenger is a separate app from Facebook so you will need to download it to your smartphone.

Messenger works like the texting feature on most smartphones. Since you generally don't want to give out personal information such as your phone number in your listing, Messenger is an easy way to communicate in Marketplace. Once you have finalized the transaction details with your customer and have made arrangements to meet with them to complete the sale, then you can give them your number if you want to or if they ask for it.

Sales can be completed without giving out your phone number though. I only give my number to a customer if they ask for it right before we meet in person. Sometimes people don't have a good internet connection with Facebook when they are on their way to meet you and aren't able to communicate through Messenger. That is a time when it might become necessary to give them your phone number. Don't put it in the listing though where anyone can see it. Send it to them in a private message through Messenger.

Be Prompt

Responding promptly to communications from buyers is an important aspect of completing the sale. When someone contacts you about an item, go ahead and respond to them as quickly as you can. You need to remember that you might not be the only one selling that type of item. There may be other individuals selling the same thing that you are, and they might respond to buyers more quickly than you do. If you are the first one to get back with the buyer (and they are happy with the price, quality, and specifics of your item), then you are more likely to be the one who gets the sale.

Your response time is actually a factor in how Marketplace evaluates your performance. It keeps track of how quickly you respond to customers and lets them know if you typically respond promptly to messages.

Be Polite

Treating people with respect and being polite will help ensure a favorable experience for both you and the buyer. Remember that you can't see the customer's facial expressions or know what they are thinking so think about what you are texting and make sure it does not come across as rude or pushy. You are sizing each other up at the same time and all they have to judge you on are the words in your text messages.

Take the time to review your messages before you send them. Sometimes you may type something incorrectly and sometimes the autocorrect feature on your phone will change what you are trying to say.

Another thing to keep in mind is that it may be the buyer's first time purchasing on Marketplace. They might be nervous or hesitant about dealing with a stranger. They might be worried about being taken advantage of. They also might not be that familiar with technology and may have a hard time communicating. Make sure you treat them with the dignity and respect that you would want in return.

Be Assertive

While you do need to be prompt and polite, you will also need to be assertive. Be sure you clearly suggest a time and place to meet to purchase the item. Suggest a time that works best for you. You may need to change it in order to work with their schedule. If they can't meet until the following week, it is okay to tell them that if someone else comes along that can meet sooner, then you are going to sell it to the other person. However, if you feel like the person you are communicating with is the best potential buyer then you can be more flexible with waiting a few days to meet with them.

Agree on a Price

Most buyers like to negotiate. This is the reason why you set your price a little bit higher than what you are willing to accept. Occasionally you will get a buyer who will just pay your asking price, but most enjoy the feeling that they have saved a little bit of money.

You need to make sure that both parties have agreed on the final price before you meet to complete the sale. You don't want to show up to the sale and have the buyer try to get you to come down on the price when you are finally meeting in person.

Discuss Payment Options

Before meeting with your customer, make sure that they are clear on which forms of payment you will accept. Obviously, you should state this in your listing, but you may also want to remind them when communicating with them prior to meeting in person. Remember, people don't always pay attention to the details in a listing.

I prefer that my customers pay for their items with cash. You can accept payments through PayPal, Venmo, Zelle, or other payment apps if you choose, but I prefer the simplicity of cash. Most buyers bring the exact payment with them, but you may want to have some change on hand in case they do not. If they don't have the exact payment and you are meeting at a store parking lot, you can always suggest that they go inside and make a small purchase in order to get change. I have had many customers do this.

If you are used to conducting your business on Etsy or eBay, then you are familiar with the potential disadvantages of using online payment services. When using services such as PayPal, you can run the risk of a dishonest buyer receiving your item and then issuing a chargeback and demanding their money back. Unfortunately, PayPal usually sides with the buyer so you could end up losing the money that they paid you. I have not had that happen to me, but I still don't want to take that risk.

While I do prefer cash, sometimes if it is going to be a couple of days before a customer can meet with me, then I will ask them to make a deposit of twenty to fifty percent for me to hold the item for those days using PayPal or some other source of online payment. Once we finally meet, I usually get the remaining balance in cash.

Close the Sale Quickly

Antiques can be beautiful, valuable, and a lot of fun to collect. But honestly, most of them are not necessities. We don't need that antique cuckoo clock to survive. Nor do we need an old typewriter or rare tin wind-up toy. An item you have for sale may possibly be something that someone has been looking for for years or it may be an impulse buy or a gift for a family member. This is something you need to keep in mind when communicating with buyers. If you have a potential buyer interested in your item, you want to close the sale as quickly as possible, because there is a chance that if they are an impulse shopper that they might change their mind or spend the money on something else if you don't complete the sale quickly. You want to complete that sale before they rethink their decision. You also want to complete the sale before they find something else that they like better than yours.

Impulse buyers are one type of buyer you maybe be dealing with. Another type is the serious collector, someone who may have been looking for years for an item like yours. While some antiques are rare and can be hard to find, it only takes having one other one available for sale at the same time as yours to provide competition for your item, and competition can drive down the price. As I mentioned earlier in this chapter, by responding promptly to the buyer, you are more likely to successfully complete the sale. When the buyer contacts you, try to set up a time to meet them as soon as is most convenient for both of you. You don't want to lose the sale to someone selling a similar item.

Letting potential customers know that other people are interested in your item can motivate them to meet with you sooner. While they probably already know if your item is something that is particularly rare or hard to find, mention it again in your conversation. You don't have to be pushy, but you can inform them of the scarcity of the item. You can even point out that while they might be able to find something similar on eBay or Etsy, meeting you to buy it now could save them a significant amount of money because they will not have to pay higher purchase prices or shipping costs. This can really make a difference on large, bulky items such as furniture or on things that are very fragile and hard to ship.

Make Sure it is Sold

Don't remove a listing or mark it as sold until you have completed the transaction. You may have established a great rapport with a buyer and made what you think is a concrete deal and then they just don't show up or they stop responding to your text messages. If it looks like a sale is going to go through, Marketplace gives you the option of marking the item as Pending. This will let buyers know that you are in the process of negotiating a deal or are waiting to meet a customer and that it is currently unavailable.

Continue to communicate with other potential buyers in case the one you have that is pending does not work out. If someone messages you, just tell them that you are supposed to meet a buyer on a certain date and if that does not work out, then you will let them know. It hasn't happened to me that often, but occasionally people just don't show up to purchase something and once this happens, they usually stop responding to your messages too. I recommend blocking anyone who agrees to meet but then doesn't show up. This is rude and it wastes your valuable time.

Mark Item as Sold

Once you have sold your antique and have cash in hand, go back into Marketplace and mark it as sold. Facebook will ask if you sold it on Marketplace and will want to know who the buyer was. It is up to you to decide how much information you want to share with Facebook regarding the final sale.

CHAPTER 15

Tips to Enhance Your Marketplace Experience

As you become more comfortable selling on Marketplace, you will come across ways to make the experience easier and less time consuming. Here are some tips to help you improve your experience.

How to View Someone's Ratings on Marketplace

To view a potential customer's ratings on Marketplace, scroll down in the listing to their name. If they have received any reviews/ratings, they will have a star review just below their name. You can click on the stars to see what areas their reviewers said that they excelled in. Some of the categories include punctuality, friendliness, item description, reliability, fair pricing, and response time.

Buyers (and sellers) can make their reviews private. If this is what they choose to do, you will not know what kind of reviews that they have received. Once you have completed a sale and marked the item as sold, you will have the option of reviewing the experience you had with your customer.

Remember that your customers will also be able to see your ratings. They will be able to review your performance in the same categories listed above that you use to review theirs. Keep these categories in mind because not only do they have the potential to improve your reviews, they also provide you with guidelines on what areas are most important to customers.

Choose a Relevant Category

When creating a listing, make sure you select the category that best represents the item you are selling. Sometimes a customer is looking for an extremely specific item such as an antique Victorian greeting card and they enter those words in the search bar. Other times though, they just want to see what kinds of items are available in a more general category, so they just click on a category and go through those listings.

No surprise, but most of my items are listed in the Antiques and Collectibles category. Occasionally though, if I think something might be more desirable based on the type of item it is rather than the fact that it is an antique then I might list it in another category. Furniture is a great example of an item that someone might search for in the furniture category rather than the antique category. Do a few searches yourself using different search terms and then do some category searches to see how other sellers are listing their items. This will help you decide the best way to categorize your items.

Be Patient with Buyers (Especially New Buyers)

Marketplace is a new concept for some. For those who have never shopped on Marketplace, it can be an intimidating experience. If you find yourself dealing with a first-time buyer, it may become your job to educate that individual on how the process works. The thing that I would emphasize first and foremost, is to be patient. You may need a lot of patience. New customers may be nervous or suspicious of the whole process. They may be worried about being scammed or entering an unsafe situation. By explaining how things work and patiently walking them through the process, you will not only have a happy customer, but possibly a repeat customer.

Review Your Numbers

Carefully review any numbers you enter in your listings and in your messages to potential buyers. Pay special attention to the price and measurements. You don't want to mistakenly quote a lower price than you intended to a buyer because it will be extremely difficult to get them to agree to a higher amount once you have quoted a lower price. You can always lower a price, but it is much harder to raise a price.

Local Slang

Have you ever heard (or used) the term chester drawers? I'm not sure if it is just a southern thing, but I grew up hearing the words chester drawers on a regular basis. If you are not familiar with this term, it is actually another way of saying chest of drawers. Some people simply refer to this item as a chest or dresser. If you have an old-fashioned or slang term that is popular in your area for a particular item, then you should add it to your title and description. Although it may not be grammatically accurate, it may be the term someone uses to look up an item so you will want to include it in your listing.

How to Block Someone on Marketplace

Occasionally, you will have a customer who has become difficult to work with. Maybe they are pushing too hard for you to lower your price or they are overly critical of the item you are selling. Maybe they didn't show up to purchase your item at the agreed upon time. Or perhaps something just doesn't seem right about them and you don't want to deal with them anymore. Marketplace gives you the option of blocking these specific customers.

Blocking Someone Who Has Messaged You Through Marketplace

Facebook gives you the option of blocking someone who has messaged you through Marketplace. Once you block them on Marketplace, they will also be blocked on Facebook.

Once they are blocked:

- They won't be able to see your listings on Marketplace.

- They can't send you any more messages.

- You will both still be able to see the messages you sent to each other before they were blocked.

To block someone who has messaged you through Marketplace, go to the specific listing that they have been messaging you about.

1. Scroll to the bottom of that screen and you will see their named listed under chats. Click on their name.

2. Marketplace will take you to a list of the messages that you have sent to each other. Click on the person's name (again) at the top of the screen.

3. This will take you to their Commerce Profile. There is a button with three dots in it just below their picture. Click on that button.

4. Click Block.

5. Click Block again on the next screen.

Hiding Your Listings from Your Facebook Friends

There are other reasons you might want to block someone from seeing your listings. Sometimes you may not want a particular person to see something that you are trying to sell. Maybe it is someone from the estate sale company that you bought the item from, or possibly a nosey neighbor or friend who always comments on your listings, or maybe you just don't want a particular friend to know your business.

You can hide your listings from your Facebook friends by simply clicking one button. Scroll to the bottom of the New Listing screen. You will see a heading called Choose Privacy Settings. By clicking on the Hide from friends option, you will be able to hide the listing from all of your Facebook friends. It will still be visible to other people on Facebook, but your Facebook friends won't be able to see it.

A disadvantage of hiding your listings from your friends is that once you do this, you are no longer able to list your items for sale in Facebook groups. This can greatly limit the number of interested people who might see your listing.

Facebook is constantly changing what you can and cannot do with Marketplace. At one time you could hide your listings from specific friends but not all of your friends. It would be nice if that were still the case because oftentimes you really only have one or two friends that you don't want to see your listings.

Facebook is Constantly Making Changes

I wrote this book to provide guidelines for selling antiques on Marketplace. One thing you need to keep in mind though is that Facebook is constantly making changes to Marketplace. I had to update several sections during the time I was writing this book because Facebook changed how some things worked. As a general rule though, Facebook has made the listing and selling process fairly simple and if (and when) they do change things, they generally make the new process easy to understand. The information about selling antiques should stay the same, but the step-by-step processes for using Marketplace and the available features may change.

When I wrote the first draft of this book, I included a chapter on how to use tags. I had to take it out before I published it because Marketplace no longer offers this option. I also included information on how to block specific Facebook friends when creating a listing. Now, Marketplace only allows you to hide your listing from all of your friends, not just specific ones.

CHAPTER 16

CONCLUSION

Well, that's it. Selling on Marketplace is a fairly easy thing to do once you get the hang of it. It is a great way to sell those items that you need to get rid of quickly or that you are just tired of having in your antique booth or eBay or Etsy shops. Once you make your first few sales, you may even decide to move all of your antique inventory to Marketplace.

Once you start selling on Marketplace on a regular basis, some of your buyers may decide to follow you on Marketplace and become frequent customers. This can provide a tremendous boost to your business. I actually have customers who ask me to try and locate specific things for them. Having repeat customers will enable you to grow your business even faster (or sell out of your current inventory if that is your goal).

While some rare and unusual items are still better suited for eBay or Etsy, many antiques and vintage items will do well on Marketplace. Through trial and error, you will determine which venue will work best for the items that you are selling.

The financial benefits of selling on Marketplace are excellent. I remember when I closed my antique booth and switched a lot of my business to Marketplace. It was such a relief not having to spend so much money on booth rentals each month. It always annoyed me that I had to sell hundreds of dollars' worth of items before I could even start making a profit. With Marketplace, the money I make is mine and I don't have to share it with an antique store.

I hope you found the information in this book to be useful and that you decide to give Marketplace a try. It is a growing market, and it is a great place for selling antiques. You can keep it simple and stick to your local market or you can join groups that have members from across the country (and around the world) and greatly expand your business. What you do with it is completely up to you.

THANK YOU

Thank you for purchasing The Antique Dealer's Guide to Facebook Marketplace: Selling Vintage and Antiques on Marketplace. I wish you much success as you use Marketplace to increase sales in your antique business. Please visit my website Southern Style Southern Charm (www.southernstyle-southerncharm.com) if you would like to follow my journey as I buy and sell antiques.

Made in United States
North Haven, CT
27 November 2022

27375576R00065